Modern Software Sales Engineering

Engineering

It isn't all just ping pong and beer

A guide to hiring or being the best Sales Engineer at a
software company

Gregory Hanson

Gregory Hanson
https://www.linkedin.com/in/gregoryhanson1

First Printing: April 2016
CreateSpace

ISBN-13: 978-1530739820

Dedicated to:

My beautiful wife and three loving children who inspire me to be greater each day. Especially my daughter Maeve, because the majority of this book was written from the hospital after you were born.

To my fantastic staff when I wrote this. The best group of Sales Engineers someone could ask for. You made my job the easiest management position ever by being the most professional and dedicated SEs around.

And to Paul and Justin. Thank you both for helping me with my first foray into the world of Sales Engineering and setting me on the path of the best career ever.

Page left intentionally blank

TABLE OF CONTENTS

Another one left blank on purpose

MODERN SOFTWARE

SALES ENGINEERING

FORWARD

Welcome to the Modern Software Sales Engineering guide to hiring and being the best Software Sales Engineers in the industry. My name is Gregory (Gregg) Hanson, self-promoter and trainer of the best Sales Engineers this side of the Mississippi. Since this is a book you can read it on either side, giving that boast immediate credibility.

You are reading this book. That tells me you are either a Sales Engineer currently, have been asked to hire an SE, or are looking to get into this career and want to know what it is all about. Either way you are here to gain more insight into what Sales Engineering is, how it works, and how to get the most out of it.

WHO SHOULD READ THIS

This book is written for anyone interested in the craft of Sales Engineering for software companies. **Note**: There are many types of Sales Engineers for computer hardware, network infrastructure, even manufacturing and civil engineering. While some of these topics may be useful to all, we are going to be discussing SEs from the point of view of selling software. Where is the software world going? Software-as-a-Service, better known as SaaS! There will be a lot of talk about renewals and success, prospects, opportunities (opps), etc. Unfortunately, that does not narrow down the scope. Everyone has their own view on what a Software Sales Engineer is.

Right now you can search for jobs titled 'Sales Engineer' and come up with thousands of postings, each with extremely different expectations for the job. Some want people comfortable working with APIs, building database schemas, a background in security, history developing websites, or mobile apps. You find everything from "Sales Engineer – No experience needed" to "Sales Engineer – 30 years mobile app dev experience required." Everyone wants something different, but they are all looking for a "Sales Engineer". Odd right?

The main sections of the book are regarding hiring and managing your first SE; what do you need, who you should hire, where can you find them. I wrote it after my creation of the Sales Engineer Quadrant, which needs a better name. Essentially it is a quadrant grid that helps you figure out what type of SE you need based on the complexity of your product and your trial volume. Even if you aren't in the position of hiring or managing these teams, I have written the sections in a way that will help you identify if you are that type of SE and what you can do to be a rockstar.

The second half of the book is filled with my appendices about being a Sales Engineer. Here you will find my take on the nuts and bolts of Sales Engineering. From learning to craft a value-based demo to tips and tricks for web presentations, there is a fount of knowledge on actually being in the field.

The material will be useful no matter what end of the spectrum you are, player, player/coach, coach, sales rep, etc.

Everyone I meet hears the same thing from me; presentation skills are king. It really doesn't matter if presenting stuff is a major component of your job, it is still one of the more important. The majority of successful people can get up in front of a group and present their thoughts in a way that everyone can understand. Presenting also happens to be the base of what Sales Engineering is all about. Everyone wins.

ONE SALES ENGINEER'S JOURNEY

I have been engineering sales for the better part of my career. The best part is that I had been doing it well before I knew that Sales Engineer was a title someone could have. It wasn't until one of the best sales directors I have ever worked for realized what was going on and said eight words that forever changed my life.

My career started as many SEs have, in support. Tech support came naturally to me as it was a cross between my two greatest skills, technology and talking to people. Always the showman, I just couldn't get jazzed up my development degree. Everyone in my undergrad was spending all their time, free and schooling, focused on coding. Friday night, coding.

Saturday morning, sleeping in. Sunday afternoon, coding. Sunday evening, coding for homework.

Not me. I was never content to sit behind a computer screen for hours to solve a puzzle and then celebrate quietly and alone. I needed to be talking to people, be out and about, being the center of attention. That bled into a burgeoning career on stage as an operatic Tenor. Managing a tech support team by day, schlepping it across states for rehearsals at night, glamorous right?

The thrill of being on stage is invigorating for me. I used that fervor for being in the spotlight to start presenting talks at conferences, or leading training seminars at local business groups. The excitement that comes from bringing a new idea to someone and having a great conversation wasn't happening on my monthly rollup of support metrics or in listening to irate customers yell at me about functionality our software didn't have. Needless to say, I was less than motivated with the prospect of a career running support teams. Then one day it happened, Sales Engineering found me.

Being the manager of the support department at a small email marketing provider did grant me some level of skill. Most of that skill involved the use of the product we sold and figuring out how to skirt around problematic areas. I also spent a lot of time talking to people about how they used email and the specific problems they were facing. One enterprising sales rep saw this, and the spark hit him, have me talk to prospects about using our tool before they purchase. If I could help them out earlier, maybe they would be more likely to buy and renew.

He approached me with the idea and since, like most managers, I had nothing better to do, I agreed. It turned out to be fun too! I was talking to people who were excited about the potential of using our tool to solve their business problems, not maddened by a support case. Then we started closing more deals and, much like a bad care of vampirism, the hunger took me. More often than not the prospects liked what I had to say, and was swaying their decision to purchase our platform over the competition. Finally, one day a prospect on the phone told me:

> *"That was the best software presentation I've ever seen. We'll get you the PO this afternoon."*

My first "on the call close"! From there my sales rep went on to become the most successful at the company by far. Somewhere around 250% of quota, which I'm told is pretty good. In no way can I take credit for his amount of success, he is an amazing sales guy by himself. However, I bolstered his efforts to close more deals by helping pre-sales than when I was just closing tickets.

Other sales reps cottoned on, and before I knew it, I was crushing through demos for prospects, and the company was growing like crazy. Every time I talked to a lead about our software the opp was nearly twice as likely to close. All the reps wanted me talking to every live person they got on the phone.

After more than a year this process really took off. I couldn't handle the volume, though. Running support as my primary duty was still taking its toll and I was doing a lot of demos. With my calendar maxed out, I finally went to the Director of Sales and told him that doing both roles was no longer possible. There was no way that I could effectively run the support department and continue to do 20-30 demos a week. Plus, selfishly, I was helping the salespeople make a lot of money and was not seeing the monetary benefit of that extra effort. I offered to teach them how to use the product so that they could demo the tool and I would go back to my hovel in support. That is when it happened, those eight magic words:

"I want you to be my demo monkey."

After he explained that he wanted me to transition full time to the sales team as a "Sales Engineer" I could not wait to get started. No more support duties, no more escalations, just the fun part of my job. On top of dropping support, I would get commission sharing?!?! My mind exploded when I found out this was actually a job people are paid to do. Hadn't I been doing that my whole life? Finding a nifty piece of software, (usually a video game) and then having a passionate discussion with people about the benefits that software brings? I had found nirvana; it was the perfect mix of my stage skills, my passion for talking to people, love for a spirited debate, and technology.

Since that fateful day, I have focused my efforts on uncovering every aspect of this extraordinary career that is still relatively new. Every software company realizes that they need a Sales Engineer, but most have not a clue on where to start. Some don't even realize that they already have a support person performing those tasks in the background. They just need that smart sales guy to point it out to them.

In this book I am going to talk about the different types of Sales Engineers, there are, how to know what you need, how to build those teams, and even how to do it. All of this information is taken from many years of being an on-the-ground SE, running different SE departments, and multiple conversations with other individuals in my shoes. Whether you are that kid in support doing demos, or a sales manager being tasked with finding a tech resource, you will get something out of this book, guaranteed.

PART ONE

THE SALES ENGINEERING GRID

THE SALES ENGINEER GRID

Welcome to the entire reason this book was born. I came up with the SE quadrant while writing an article about the main different types of Sales Engineers. Each company has needs and opinions on what SEs should do. With every job posting there are wildly diverse expectations; long proof of concepts, POCs for short, vs. "try and buy", highly technical vs. super easy, low volume or high. The problem was trying to figure out the common themes connecting them.

New photo

scans

(Completed)

My time as a Sales Engineer so far has been split between two different companies. The first was selling a SaaS email solution, very easy to use, inexpensive, high volume trials. My week consisted of around 30 stock demos. Some amount of discovery was done during the call, but it was mostly just a rote demo. We tried to get as many qualified leads into demos as possible to help people understand the unique values that we brought and gave them a chance to ask some questions. Better than a recording but very time-consuming.

Afterward, I moved to a company that was, due to being a more enterprise tool, doing lesser volume of trials but was still relatively easy to get started with. We averaged ten demos a week which gave me plenty of time to customize the demos based on the information Sales had gathered. There was also a good amount of technical follow-up and ongoing conversations about particular values. I was still engineering sales, but there was a very different approach.

Looking at the two companies, I realized that the only real change was volume. One inexpensive tool and one enterprise level tool, both relatively easy to use, and yet the SE strategy had to be modified. The first needed rapid fire demos for a short sales cycle, and the latter required a more custom nuanced approach to the demo for a longer sales cycle. With my new found knowledge my trusty yellow notepad came out, and I sketched what is arguably the most influential diagram of Sales Engineering in the industry.

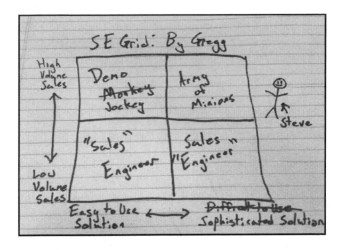

GAZE AT ALL THE ARTISTIC WONDER

Drawing the quadrant clarified to me how different companies employ their SE group. The intersection of volume and solution is what directs the type of SE you want. Some people will say "What is the point of the Demo Jockey, a sales heavy SE is the way to go!". That would be awesome! Go to your boss and say that you need to hire four high-priced SEs to cover one lower cost demo jockey and get back to me. Don't worry I'll wait.

You can't just jump into the world of Sales Engineering with a massive department. It needs to grow organically and scale appropriately. Building out all the assets for an SE to be successful doesn't happen overnight. Yes, eventually you will modify the group as your company evolves; you just need to start somewhere first.

Any of the three named types are perfect for a first SE depending on your current situation. The next few chapters go into detail on each category, but the basic outline is:

- **Demo Jockey**:
  - High volume demos for an easy to use product
  - Stock demos that show values and let prospects ask questions
- **"Sales" Engineer**
  - Technical asset but heavy on the soft skills
  - Ideal for highly customized demos and being the technical manager for the buying cycle
- **Sales "Engineer" or Solution Architect**
  - In-depth technical mastery of setting up the product for customers, build integrations, etc.
  - Still salesy enough to do discovery and give presentations to C-Suite
- **Army:**
  - Where you need a bit of everything
  - Mostly reserved for large organizations, not a first SE team

Feel free to jump to the chapter that fits your group best. I recommend that you go through all of them at some point but skip around for now. Just like a 'Choose Your Own Adventure' book!

DEMO JOCKEY

The first type of Sales Engineer we will discuss is the beloved Demo Jockey, the workhorse of the SE world, doing presentations innumerable (unless you are using proper metrics). The Demo Jockey spends their days doing stock software demos for prospects. They are the highest volume of widget producing SE there is. Demo Jockeys will typically do more than 20 hour long demos per week on an ongoing basis. Some weeks may dip down slightly but on average they will be in that 20-30 range. Not that any of the SE types is 'less' than the others, but typically this is the first go around for someone as a Sales Engineer.

Spending more than half your work week on presentations naturally impacts the type of demo possible. Demo Jockey type demos are mostly rote walkthroughs of the tool. Think of it as a glorified recording, in as non-demeaning a way as possible. One cannot possibly customize each demo to the prospect's environment, spend much time doing discovery on their individual pain points, or deviate too far from the standard demo. Strict scheduling for demos will block their calendar for three to four demos back to back with no wiggle room.

On the other side of the equation is the lack of time for the Demo Jockey to work on projects outside of presentations. Typically they will not be actually designing the demos or building the demo environment, which means they are going to need a lot of support. Churning through demos for a high-velocity product is key here. Remember the Demo Jockey is most likely in their first SE position or aren't even aware they are an SE. It is likely they do not have the most refined skills for designing this type of assets.

Key Takeaways:

- **20+ demos a week average**
- **Stock demos, little customization**
- **New to their career as a Sales Engineer**

WHY YOU NEED THEM

We are starting in the upper-left of the quadrant; high volume sales with an easy and intuitive product. Most likely you are a SaaS service. Mostly web based products that require a name and email address to get access to a two or four-week trial. On top of that, your sales cycle is a quick turnaround. You grab the customer and show that value quickly, or they go with someone else. The Demo Jockey SE works best with these easy to trial, short sales cycle products. Think about this from the customer's perspective on their journey from trial to purchase, starting with the trial.

The customer gets access to your tool, and the sales team gets notified of the hot new lead. Ideally, you already have video content available online to get your prospects started. A demo should **not** be the first tool your sales team leverages down a prospect's throat. Give them time to use the product and get a base level

Sales Training

understanding of the capabilities. Without that knowledge, the demo becomes training on how to use the product, not what values your solution brings. Plus it is demotivating for your SE. When I was the Demo Jockey, I did far too many demos that started with 'What does your product do?' or 'How do I log in?'. Junk demos are part of the job, but too many and it becomes part of your previous job.

Now the prospect has used your product, built some assets, generated some questions on its use, etc. This is where the Demo Jockey comes into play. If you don't have an SE you enter the part of the sales cycle where your reps get inundated with usage-based questions or the lead goes dark. Why does this happen? Put your customer cap back on.

You are trialing a bunch of tools in a market where you can get access ten great, likely inexpensive, tools in short order. Once in you poke around, check if there is the high-level functionality you are looking for, and see if you can do 'something' with it. If the product checks off the initial boxes you are happy and go onto evaluating; maybe asking a couple of questions to the salesperson but more than likely just trialing the competition. All these products have the same features anyway, might as well find the one that is easiest to use.

Without an SE, you will catch a lot of customers. People will decide that your product does what they want in a manner that pleases them and purchase. Many will not, because they don't see the value that your solution brings. A Demo Jockey armed with a compelling story showing the five top values your product brings exposes the customer to purchasing reasons they would not see on their own. Remember, I'm looking for something easy and fast. When your SE starts telling me about pain points I have and how your app solves those problems I become intrigued, at least, intrigued enough to continue talking to your sales team.

Key Takeaways:

- **Short sales cycle for easy to use/trial app**
- **High volume inbound leads**
- **Seeing leads drop out after initial download**

How to Find Them

So you figured out that your first Sales Engineer should be the Demo Jockey. First: congratulations! Second: time to get hiring! Where do you start looking and what qualities are you looking for? Unfortunately, you are not looking for people who are engineering sales currently. Most likely you are looking for individuals who have never heard of Sales Engineering and do not know it is an option. Now you have the two-fold task of finding qualified candidates and convincing them this is the career of choice.

Fortunately, there are a lot of established positions from which SEs can be plucked. Most notorious for the Demo Jockey is the humble support engineer. Tech Support, Customer Service, Support Team, Steve, whatever you call them, your support team is the best place to look for your first Demo Jockey.

Support Steve is already an expert in your product and likely the industry. He already knows the value your product brings because he is helping people get at those values daily. Further, an unfortunate part of support, they are used to repetitive tasks. They close ticket after ticket, likely with many of the same issues. Product expertise plus a proven ability to do high volume tasks daily is an excellent starter.

Support people do not take offense at the next comment. I myself started my career as tech support and moved up to running support teams. Support is the unsung hero at most companies. However, support is not the most enjoyable, respected, or well-payed profession. People never call support just to say 'everything is going alright!'. When times are tough, the support people know their jobs are on the line. Sales is a fast-paced, fun, and generally much more lucrative environment. The gregarious support staff member is a great fit for your first Demo Jockey, even if they don't know it. Give them a path out of support to a more visible and visceral part of the organization. Show them that there is a career outside of closing tickets; because if you have to be closing something, close sales.

If there isn't a lively pool of candidates in your support organization, you can look at others. Professionals who have been working for two to four years in software support are some of the most ideal Demo Jockeys. Just make sure you find one with that showman personality and you are set.

Key Takeaways:

- **Outgoing support staff make the best Demo Jockeys**
- **Internal promotions look great to the CEO**
- **Demo Jockey candidates are generally younger in their career**

HOW TO TRAIN THEM

Demo Jockeys are a particular breed of Sales Engineer that tends to need less training and more assets. Training is critical for every staff member in an organization. The Demo Jockey needs it as well as structure due to the more junior level of this position. First, you will need to tackle giving them the tools to succeed; the second is training on how to get there.

For the tools portion, your first Demo Jockey needs two main areas to cover: the value-based demo script and the environment with which to perform said demo. Focus on the script first. Even without the demo environment, you will need to know what your story is so that an environment can be crafted appropriately. The script should not be training or tutorial but a value-based story. When people leave the demo, you want them recalling four to six values that your product brings, not 100 steps on how to do it.

For help on this refer to the 'Tell-Show-Tell' section in the appendices section.

If you have pulled from your support team, then they are more than capable of creating an environment to highlight the features for you, especially when armed with your demo script. Keep the environment as close to a real-world scenario as possible. Allow your demo viewers to imagine themselves incorporating the values you are presenting into their lives. Save this environment however you can. Keep it stored in a way that every day, or even every demo, can be reverted to an unblemished state.

Once you have your assets and your Demo Jockey is reading the scripts you have provided, it is time to begin presentation training. Generally, your Demo Jockey will not have prior public speaking experience and may be shy about presenting at all. Help them get over this by giving their demo to you in a conference room about once a week to start. Record the session and then have them go listen to themselves. While they are listening, ask them to focus on one piece, their voice. Do they modulate their tone at all or is it a flat recitation? Let them become familiar with their speaking style.

After they have listened to a couple of their own demos and understand how their voice works, have them present to you again. Now have them pretend it is just a simple conversation. Encourage them to have an ebb and flow to their voice. Push them towards normal speaking cadence, pauses in their delivery, excitement during significant value props, etc. Once they have pinpointed how to do that, a simple demo review once per week will allow each of you to refine further which part of the demo needs more variation of pitch and speed.

Key Takeaways:

- **Provide both a script and a demo environment**
- **After your demo environment is built, add the exact clicks into your script**
  - **This becomes training material for future Demo Jockeys**
- **Presentation skills – Start with incorporating basic conversational ebbs and flows to the demo**

How to Manage and Measure Them

Demo Jockeys are workhorses. They are running 20-30 hour long demos per week, filling up the vast majority of their calendar. The biggest challenge I have found running a Demo Jockey team is keeping them out of the quagmire of overbooking. Burnout happens in this job, and we need to work to keep that from happening. With an open calendar that the Sales team has access to every free moment will be filled.

Even though this is a high volume tasked position, you have to remember they are people. Six straight demos back to back with a half hour break followed by two more demos will wreck anyone. Days will happen when you need to buckle down and work through it but they should be the exception.

Empower your SE to manage their calendar to their comfort level. Personally, I do not like to do more than two demos back to back without a short break.

Make sure they know they can block an hour for lunch, 15-minute breaks if they have several back to back calls, etc. Put a hard cap on the number of demos they can do in a day at six so that they are never booked solid from start to finish. These open times are perfect for catching up on emails to the sales team and prospects.

Managing the schedule is the largest task. Second biggest is accurately reporting on what your new SE is doing so that you can prove value. For the Demo Jockey, this is relatively straightforward. A straight line metric on demos done will give you everything that you need. From that data you should be looking at the following points with relevant reasons listed:

- **Trends in demo usage for peak seasons**
    - ○ Gain insight into staffing schedule to maintain full staff during busy times
- **Close ratio of opps with demos vs. no demo**
    - ○ Show how much more likely an opp is to close with SE intervention
- **Revenue attached to closed opps with a demo**
    - ○ Value each SE brings to the team
- **Average revenue gained per SE engagement**
    - ○ Judgement on minimum opp size to leverage SEs vs. recorded demos

Of course, there are many other bits of information you can glean from the data. However, the above are the most common to start looking at. Giving your new SE team a value boost to the higher-ups is exactly what you need to turn your new SE into a new SE department.

Key Takeaways:

- Empower staff to manage their calendars to prevent burnout
- Track every demo against an opportunity to show real value of team
- Demo Jockeys are people too

"Sales" Engineer

Moving down the quadrant we find ourselves talking about the "Sales" Engineer. To avoid overuse of quotes in this chapter, we will refer to the "Sales" Engineer as plain old Sales Engineer. Innovative I know, but with all the different titles of SEs, this quadrant matches up best with the term Sales Engineer. Engineering sales is the primary task of this SE. Typically they are not doing POCs, architecting product features for prospects, training customers, building integrations, etc. They should be capable of those activities just not necessarily specializing in them. SEs are specialists in Sales with a focus on charismatic presentations.

Since they focus on presentations, you would think they are crushing through demos like the Demo Jockey. You would be incorrect. I'm sorry.

Concentrating on their presentations means they are spending much more time preparing for their demos and customizing each one to the needs of the prospect. It doesn't always need to be a 1:1 ratio of prep time to demo, but this type of SE should be maxing out at 15-20 demos on a heavy week and averaging somewhere around 10. Coincidentally my department is 100% Sales Engineers who averaged out to two calls per work day last year.

Our Sales Engineer loves the sales process and is hungry for the hunt. During their presentations, they are able to seed in values of the product, challenges for the competition, and also gather critical data that people generally do not tell the sales rep.

The SE is your ace in the hole, able to build near instant rapport with prospects and become a trusted technical advisor. Sometimes they do it with a few jokes about the sales rep. Regardless they are the reps partner who is acting on behalf of the customer. Juxtaposition or double agent? You decide.

Key Takeaways:

- Ten demos per week on average
- High customization for each presentation and lots of follow up
- Charismatic presenter with an eye for the sale

WHY DO YOU NEED THEM?

You live in a world where your sales cycle is relatively short (1-3 months), your product is easy to use, and you aren't overwhelmed with the volume of leads with respect to your workforce. The sales team spends a good amount of time on each lead walking them through their current pain points and how we are going to solve them. Trials are mostly self-led; you don't build POCs or handle integrations for the prospect.

The tool is easy enough that they can get going with it but is more important to review in their environment. "Is it cheap and does it work" is not sufficient in this case. Now you know you need a Sales Engineer.

Typical companies that would start with a Sales Engineer look like Salesforce.com for a business that needs 25 seats (back 10-15 years ago before they were huge. They qualify for the army of minions now.).

They aren't building custom integrations, or even setting up the environment for those accounts, merely exposing the value.

This will probably be an essential component of each of the sections. Once the prospect activates their trial, a demo should **not** be the first trick a rep uses. Too often sales reps try to use a demo as free starter training. First, make your product easy to use so that anyone can figure it out. Second, make self-service content to help them with the more advanced stuff.

The SE demo should focus on value, not how-tos. It is much easier for a lead, who is likely evaluating other software that has the same functionality for the same price, to remember five fundamental values rather than 100 tutorial steps.

Here we begin to veer away from the high volume process of the Demo Jockey. In this world, your product is technical enough that your salespeople shouldn't be expected to know everything. Unless you have technical account managers, it is too much to expect your sales team to be able to effectively split their time between sales activities and maintaining expertise in your product and industry. Should they be able to do a high level five minute walkthrough?

Totally! Should they also be expected to understand the full implementation of your product and the intricacies of your competition? Not so much. Now you introduce your Sales Engineer to buttress their efforts.

Sans SE you are probably getting a lot of questions from your prospects that have to be escalated to support or development. There are usually critical business pain points that are technical enough that a salesperson may not understand how it would relate to your product. Either way, there is a lot of information that is 'over the head' of the sales rep, and that is missed value when no SE is listening in.

Editor's Note: I love sales people. They are some of my best friends. It isn't bad that they don't understand the tech stuff, they specialize in Sales! Personally, I am not an Olympic athlete. I don't get offended when people look at someone other than me for deals that require Greco-Roman wrestling to close. You bring in a specialist.

Key Takeaways:

- Product is not overly technical but more involved than just 'plug and play'
- Most POCs, integrations, etc., are handled by the prospect or partners
- Lots of technical questions from prospects getting escalated to support or dev teams
- I am not a great Greco-Roman wrestler or really any other type of wrestling

HOW TO FIND THEM

There is no one true and best Sales Engineer other than the one that works best for your organization. Great Sales Engineers should be able to be the best at many organizations regardless of what they need. Even still, the Demo Jockey is one type of SE that is an excellent breeding ground for all others. As discussed in the previous chapter the Demo Jockey is generally in their first SE position. After a couple of years cutting their teeth a Demo Jockey should be ready to begin specializing in one branch of the SE career. Assuming you don't have a full department of Demo Jockeys to pull from you generally will be better off looking for an outside hire.

The two places that will give you the most success of an internal hire are Support and, surprisingly, Sales. You will want to look for someone further into their career regardless of what they are doing. These SEs need to have enough business experience to understand pain points have been exposed to different levels of an organization, and general experience with a sales process.

Support team leaders or managers have the technical background and may be wondering what is next for their career. Potentially there is a salesperson that always had a knack for the product and enjoys working with the product more than making cold calls. Those people are good prospects to give some presentation training to and get them on the phone!

Alternately you can begin to look at other Sales Engineers. This is a risky proposition, but the reward could be great. Especially if this is your first SE, you will want someone with general experience creating demos and other assets. Don't think that you can just have your marketing team whip something up either. This needs to be a carefully crafted story of value. The downside comes from being set in their ways. Even if they aren't aware of it, an SE is going to fall back into what they know best. What they know best is their previous company's demo. You should be prepared to help them unlearn their old process and learn the new one. At the very least you will need to work with them to craft a demo that works for your product and audience.

Regardless of where you look, you will need to find a candidate with a strong ability to discuss technical topics with both tech and non-tech audiences, a great personality over the phone and sales acumen. My ideal candidates are strong in one of the big three "Sales, Technical, and Presentation", with entry-level experience with the other two. Think of an existing inside sales rep that dabbles in scripting on the side and is Dungeon Master for their D&D campaign. Sales experience and the base knowledge of tech and presentation. Don't look at just their existing job skills. Find out what they do for fun. They are people whose outside-of-work skills may directly contribute to being an SE. Personally, I came from Tech Support. I am also a professional Opera singer (presentation) and am able to convince people that Opera is a valid career choice (sales).

Key Takeaways:

- Demo Jockeys internally or externally are great candidates
- Sales Engineers with 1-2 years' experience are great but may need retraining
- Ensure that someone can create a value-based demo for the new SE

HOW TO TRAIN THEM

One advantage to the Sales Engineer is that you (should) already have 50% of the training setup. Send them to your sales training! Your Sales Engineer needs to be fully versed in your selling methodology. Sandler, Challenger, Customer Centric, Door-to-Door, etc., you want your SE to understand exactly what the sales people are doing. Not because the SE will be selling but to better understand where they can be most effective! This has the dual role of some team bonding with Sales and inheriting some sales tips.

When your SE knows that the sales rep is trying to figure out the before scenarios the customer is experiencing they will know better which questions to ask. The more symbiosis between them the better they will be able to play off each other during a call. Remember, prospects trust a good SE and will gladly tell them how many team members will need the product after dodging that question from the rep for weeks. You are better off arming your Sales Engineer to partner with your reps instead of just coming in rogue.

Regardless if you do weekly lunch trainings, yearly/quarterly off-sites, random emails of quotes from sales leaders, have this SE be in lock step with your reps. The SE gets the full benefits of the training, and your reps will be able to gain some insight from how an SE approaches problems. Be cognizant on both sides; if you are doing sessions on territory planning let your SE leave early. If you are doing training on how to do the elevator pitch or role plays, get your SE involved and pass on some presentation skills!

As I mentioned earlier, the sales training is half of what you need. The second half is presentation training. Sales Engineers need to be smooth on the phone and understand how to hold a conversation no matter who is on the other end. This may be a bigger challenge if you are not a great presenter yourself. Luckily you are reading this book, and I have included several appendices on presentation skills. Of all the skills though you should have them focus on, my favorite and the one I find most effective is the 'Tell-

Show-Tell' method. It allows you to craft your demo in a way that the presentation is useful for showing value instead of features.

In lieu of those specifics however, there are a couple of great boons that you can do for your SE. Think of them like a Doctor. They never will master their craft but will forever be practicing. Except if they mess up people just are a little bored, not a little dead. What that means is they need **opportunities to practice,** and there is no lack of chances to present. Get them doing training videos and webinars for marketing, then make them watch it. Pay for their ToastMasters club membership at a local chapter. Have them give the sales team training when new features are released. The biggest part here is to get them comfortable speaking in front of a computer and a group of people. Once they are comfortable enough they can begin to take steps to improve their ability to speak. If you really want to go for the gold, bring in an Improv Comedy trainer for your whole team and have the SE help lead it. The fireworks will be fantastic.

Key Takeaways:

- Involve the SE fully in your existing sales training regimen
- Invest in presentation training, ToastMasters dues, public speaking classes, etc.
- Force the SE into any opportunity to present live or via remote sessions/recordings

How to Manage and Measure Them

Metrics for the Sales Engineer are more sophisticated than the Demo Jockey but much less complex than the Sales "Engineer". I stick by my thought that activities are the top widget to measure. Monitor your SEs presentations against opportunities and you will get excellent information. The key is to get all the data and then pull information from that data. Data points to track closely are:

- Demos against Opportunities
- Discovery calls against Leads/Opps
- Requests-for-Proposals/Information (RFP and RFIs) against Opps
- Pretty much any call with a customer or prospect against their relevant account info

One big piece about the data is that you need to collect **all** the pertinent data so that you can extract information from it. That is where your opp data comes into play. Chance of closing, information missing, deal size, length of time open, etc., are all points that your SE data needs to fulfill its goal. Remember that the only reason an SE is on the phone with a prospect is to further the deal. Why would you waste SE resources on a lead if there is no opportunity there, and why would you spend time on a call if it won't push the deal closer to the sale? Answer: You shouldn't.

Now that you have all this great data it is time to pull your info. Some top information you should be gleaning include:

- How likely is an SE call to push a deal into the next stage
- How often does an SE assisted discovery call turn into an opp
- Revenues generated per SE activity
- Length of time average closed won opp takes from creation to demo, then demo to close

The best part about getting this information is not just to have it and spout of details but to make decisions! Using this info you will be able to know the best time in the sales cycle to leverage a demo, what opps just won't benefit from an SEs time, or how much time an SE should spend on an RFI/RFP. Staffing decisions will also become easier. Once you have one SE running at peak efficiency on the right deals, you can easily show the Master of Coin when you need to get a new one and how quickly they will pay for themselves!

Of course, this is my take on metrics. The biggest piece of advice I can give is to dutifully metric everything that your SE does, marketing content, trade shows, ping pong games, etc. It is not a horrible task to ask them to do, and it gives you the ability to correlate that data as needed. Especially since as your team grows you can do statistical analysis on every aspect of their job. Then when you need to make a decision you can say 'We need X because of these facts' instead of 'I want to do this for reasons.' Directors love fact-based decisions; nobody likes decisions made because of your gut feeling, except your gut.

Key Takeaways:

- Measure everything – When you need the information you want the data available
- Use the data to make your decisions on appropriate SE usage
- Make sure to track data points against relevant opp data to gather all possible info

SALES "ENGINEER"

We are venturing towards the right half of the SE grid now with a low volume but…. 'sophisticated' offering. Since your product involves more setup and technical prowess to get started, you need the Sales "Engineer". Typically you will find these people called Systems Engineers, Sales Consultants, or Solution Architect. We will use Solution Architect here because the name fits this quadrant best in my not so humble opinion. It's my book; I get to decide the title we go with. These SEs are still engineering sales but are doing a lot more on the engineering half of the field. They really are building out the solution that the prospect buys.

The esteemed Solution Architect spends their days working in depth with prospects getting the application setup and running correctly. Sometimes this is a lengthy proof of concept for enterprise deals where the SE goes onsite and sets up the whole environment, training as they go. Other positions are building light integrations between your product and the prospect's environment before showing a real world demo. Either way the SE spends a significant amount of their week building custom environments or integrations for prospects. They may do as few as one or two prospects a month, but more than likely would start around five engagements per week.

At this point, we break away from calling what they do a 'demo' and focus on engagements. Yes, they will still be doing demos; they will just be doing way more prep than demoing. Prep will likely include a lot of discovery with prospects, back and forth during setup, and reviews to ensure the scope of the project is aligned with what the prospect is looking to do. That is a lot more than just a demo, and frankly, one of the most difficult types of SEs there is.

You may already have people in your organization doing this effort. It is usually taking place at the close of the sale and through the onboard process under the guise of professional services. The prospect buys and then you get them setup and running. Imagine a world where your prospects get setup and running first? How much more likely are they to purchase then? But we can't just have a staff of developers working on projects that may not result in a sale, can we?!? No! You **can** have a group of SEs do it though.

Key Takeaways:

- Around five prospect engagements per week that culminate in a highly custom demo
- Building integrations and setting up the environment for the customer
- One of the most technically challenging SE positions

WHY DO YOU NEED THEM?

The right side of the quadrant is dedicated to those companies that offer a more sophisticated solution. What makes it complex is not the fancy tech behind the scenes but the actual use of the tool. Think sophisticated in terms of difficult to use and implement. This is not a dig at companies that need this either. Many toolsets that fall into this category are solving very complex problems. Complex in terms of integrating several disparate systems into one managing tool, bringing wildly different departments onto one platform, or even just plain old difficult to get setup properly.

I know what you are thinking right now. Hand this goldmine to the sales people and bundle in $50k of professional services to every deal. We get deals, customers get products they need, by the time setup is done the prospect is so involved that the renewal is guaranteed! Wrong. Large companies fall into this trap all the time. Let us use a fictional company call GO. GO sells printers and software. Nobody ever got fired for purchasing GO branded software even if it failed.

GO happens to have an extensive and very highly regarded Test Management/Automation suite. They would sell massive implementations of their tools and include huge professional services packages. I theoretically have spoken with many prospects that went with their suite only to come back a year later with the same story:

"We purchased their suite expecting it to do what we wanted based on what the sales rep said. Services spent nine months getting it going and this is not helping us solve the problem we purchased it for. Now we have three months to find a replacement."

This was not due to the toolset either. GO could have a suite that was powerful and performs really well; just not as well for everyone. Sure the sales rep can sell a package, but is isn't always what the customer needs. This is precisely where the Solution Architect plays well. Get into the prospects system first, setup the environment for them, build out those first integrations, and then hit them with the sale. By getting the product prepped for the customer you are able to much more quickly show them the value of your tools because it is actually working for them! When the prospect asks for a discount now, all you need to do is turn around and show them how much XYZ they will save and ask if they really want to delay or derail this sale over 5%?

So the services team is out. Ok, fine, we will just ship this off to a dev team that can prep everything for us. No! Firstly, the dev team is busy building new functionality for you. Second, the demo still needs to happen! No offense to developers but do you want someone who spends 10-15 hours a day writing code chatting with prospects or someone trained in sales? I'll take the art of communication any day.

This is the main reason you need the blend of sales and engineering for this role. A person perfectly comfortable discussion the DB schema with the prospect, reading their API docs, building the integration, and then having a value-based discussion with the C-suite on why your solution is superior. Does this unicorn exist? I contend it does.

Basic API

Key Takeaways:

- Sophisticated solution due to implementation, integrations, breadth of use, etc.
- Product is not able to be used without heavy technical lifting
- Need someone who is comfortable building the integration as well as talking to the prospect

HOW TO FIND THEM

Unfortunately, I have not directly run a group of Solution Architects in the past. This information is based on discussions with other SE managers and SAs at other companies. However, a lot of the principles for finding any type of SE are similar. Look for a group of people who have your baseline skillset. For a Solution Architect, you need to have technical chops and a great personality. Who has the best tech skills? Developers!

Stereotypes exist because a majority of people in a group match a certain description. It isn't a bad thing! Excel at development and, generally, there is some deficiency in the soft skill department. I got a development degree back in my undergrad, and every classmate of mine was more comfortable in front of their computer than in front of people. You just have to find that one developer who has a yearning for the public eye. Good skills to look for are the devs that do feature training or are actively participating in product meetings, showing the ability to ingest the code and spit out a coherent business case to the higher ups.

All developers are different, but the ones who I have found are more likely to possess these skills, web designers. Younger people who grew up around APIs and live on the bleeding edge of new frameworks. Most of the time there tech skills will directly line up with what you need too, using APIs to build integrations and customizations for your prospects. Sacrificing a few points in the Soft Skills tree to gain a better technist is fine too. As long as they have the baseline skillset anyone can be taught to give great presentations and lead discovery sessions.

If you are having trouble recruiting a developer, there is always the professional services team. People who are already building integrations and chatting with customers can be molded to become an SE. Depending on the length that your support team goes for fixing issues; they may be a valid option to choose.

Key Takeaways:

- **Web and API developers are more likely to have a decent amount of soft skills**
- **Tech heavy professional services or support teams are likely candidates**
- **Rely more on the tech skills with a baseline in presentation**

We will be omitting the training and matrices portion of the Solution Architect mostly due to the highly personalized nature of the role. Aside from the standard presentation and sales training, your SA needs to be an expert on your product, industry, and related technologies. You are the authority on that training material, not I.

PART TWO

BEING A GREAT SALES
ENGINEER

TIPS AND TRICKS INTRO

Now that you are armed with the knowledge of what type of Sales Engineer you are (or need), it is time to get a handle on how to be the best SE you can! There are many people doing and viewing software demos every day.

Your job is to provide the best demo your prospects have ever seen or run the team that does that. People buy on emotion. You give them a demo that makes them feel good and delivers a few great values they can remember, you have done your part.

Over the next few short sections, I will break out several different components that are critical to Sales Engineering. They have been adapted from a series of articles I publish on the craft of Sales Engineering.

Each is important in its own right, but the first few are on actual SE duties (presentation techniques, tips, etc.), and the last set is on the management of your team (metrics, training, whatnot). At the very end are a few items that are generally useful, scoring rubrics, generic SE profiles. Items that I have built and used across several SE teams that help me produce the best SEs in the world.

Doing a Bad Software Demo

We have all sat in those demos. You know the ones where you start playing with your phone about 10 minutes in, just after the 20 slide generic company presentation and right before they start explaining all the options in the Edit menu. At the end of that hour you know three points:

- The name of the company
- The name of the product
- That you felt miserable for an hour because of the first two

People buy based on emotion. If their lasting emotion from your demo is sheer boredom, they will associate purchasing and using your product as adding misery to their day. Let them have fun and they will remember that your product made them happy. Personally, I would rather use tools that make me happy than miserable.

The funny part is that doing a good software demonstration is really easy. It is doing a horrible one that takes all the effort. Let us break this down and look at three components of a horrible demo (and their Bizarro world equivalent of a great one).

1) 101 Features I Know You Need!!

This is the first, and most common, attribute of a horrible software demo. We love our product. It does so many amazing things. Therefore, it is only natural that if we show all these amazing features, only a fool would be able to resist buying!

You start to see the effects of the wild ride just a few minutes in. The prospect becomes unresponsive (probably overwhelmed with how much awesome our functionality is), no questions are asked (because apparently we covered everything they could possibly want), and at the end of the demo, you never hear from them again. Well, I'm sure they will buy once the shock wears off.

Nope. All we have done is show how needlessly complicated our product is. We have also undoubtedly revealed many features that are entirely useless to the customer. Now they won't want to pay full price for all these extra features, or at worst, decide it is going to be too difficult to use and drop the evaluation.

Alternately you can show only the functionality that would be immediately useful to them. Walk them through the story of how your product would work in their environment. Show a possible future where using your software makes their job easier and their life happier.

How can you do this? Just ask a few questions. Spend two minutes asking them what their environment is like, what they are currently doing, how it is impacting their day. Now you can begin to tailor your demo to their needs, reducing the amount you need to cover, time to cover it, etc. You have treated them like a human instead of a feature dartboard.

2) Mouse Movement Marathon

We are so excited to show off the multitudinum of features that we just can't get to the next one fast enough. Our software is so easy to use that I can fly through each section, proving it! We know exactly where to go so let's get there as quickly as we can, waggle the mouse over a relevant button then move on. Fly free my demo compatriots!

Everyone does this at the start. You have done this demo a hundred times and are on auto-pilot. Unfortunately for your viewer, they only have your cursor to lead them through your demo. When you are doing a web demo, the mouse is the only motion they see. As soon as you flit your mouse to the other side of the screen their attention is left where you were, not where you went. Now they have the opportunity to start meandering around your screen looking at everything except what you are talking about. They will not be listening to you either; what they are looking at has nothing to do with your words.

Our job is to give people a guided tour of a day in their life of using our product. We need to use every effort to keep them on the boat. The easiest way to do that? Slow mouse movements. A mouse creeping slowly across the screen is instinctively followed, allowing them to join you in your story.

And for goodness sake, when you are done moving the mouse take your hand off it. I know you had five cups of coffee but we don't need to see your mouse jittering around the screen like a pinball ball. It isn't drawing my attention to that feature, it is making me sick. By moving the mouse slowly, you remove the need to try and draw their attention to your feature of interest. Also saves on carpal tunnel surgery costs.

3) Don't bother thinking until the words are out there

Vocalized. Silence.

If weeee... even let the....uhhh.. customer... ummm..... think.... that there is a...,,, pause.... in the demonstration they will....mmmm. butt in and..uhhh.... derail the whole... ... thing. Umm..... Yeah....

We vocalize our silences by drawing out words, adding crutch phrases, and the ever-valuable "Uhh." This gives us time to think about the next few words we are going to say and prevents the customer from chiming in with an annoying question. It is also a psychological way that we are communicating "Hey, I am unfamiliar with this topic and need some help." Instead, you could just pause for a second to gather your thoughts.

As awkward as you feel when doing it, pausing for a deep breath between sentences is natural. Think about the last time you were chatting with the barkeep. You didn't steamroll them until you passed out, you had a pleasant chat. Just a nice, friendly chat.

There is a natural ebb and flow of conversation and that is exactly what a demo it; a conversation about our how your product can help the user. Not only does breathing make you sound less robotic but it gives you back time! Time to think about an entire phrase. Time to prepare a concise and cogent thought about the next part of the story you are weaving. That one pause will allow you time to form the whole idea so that you don't need to take a thought break every few seconds. It makes you sound like an expert instead of someone grasping for the next word.

This will also slow down the conversation. Ensuring that people have a chance to actually process what you are saying in conjunction with what you are showing them.

Not bad eh?

There you go. Three ways to do a perfectly horrible software demo. It takes a lot of effort to fly at top speed through every feature without stopping for breath. At the same time, it is relatively easy to have a conversation about the values your product provides to a particular user. Two choices. Easy and efficient or difficult and.... well boring.

Personally, I would rather take the easy path. I mean, they only have to sit through it once. I have to live it 5 times a day. Let's make it a story that we don't mind rereading.

USING TELL-SHOW-TELL

As Sales Engineers, we tout the term 'Tell-Show-Tell' as a great demo framework. Tell 'em what they are about to see, show it to 'em, tell 'em what they saw. It allows you to easily encapsulate your demo into little digestible widgets. 'Tell-Show-Tell' is the Superman to Bizarro World's method of 'Show-Tell-Tell.' The latter of the two is the standard demo presentation where someone yells functionality at you for 45 minutes and then asks if there are any questions. Yes, can I have my 45 minutes back? No? Well, thanks for nothing Bizarro.

'Tell-Show-Tell' breaks that concept up and reorganizes it, unfortunately though the phrase itself doesn't explain what you are supposed to do. Tell them something, show it, tell them again. That seems more like 'Talk-Show-Talk'. Believe me, I can talk for hours and not make a point. It isn't very useful.

To help understand and apply this, I break it into 'Tell #1', 'Show', and 'Tell #2.' With that method, you can start to break down your demo into multiple little stories.

Tell #1 - What is the Need?

The first tell is where you are not doing anything on screen, just talking. I know that is hard people but put down the mouse and talk. Tell the viewers what functionality they are about to see and what need it fulfills. By doing this you establish what is coming, allowing the viewer to mentally prepare for information transfer. Focus on the need though, not the functionality.

This puts them in the frame of mind to internalize their problem and understand how your product fills it. It also puts a finite cap on what they are about to see. Like numbering the slides on your deck, it gives them the ability to see the end is close, no need to check out let their attentions wander wondering when you will stop shouting menu options at them. Lead them to the water, let them drink and be nourished.

Ex: "You said you have an issue losing pen caps and getting ink on your shirt. The 'Click Pen 5000' has a simple click mechanism to hide the pen nib without the need for a cap."

Show - Demo the Feature

This will be a short section and deserves a filler paragraph. Dinosaur elevator dirty monkey swing belt. That should suffice.

Now you head into the demo portion where you show your functionality. The tip here is to avoid narrating what you are doing. When you say 'click here, do this, push that, etc.', the 'Show' section becomes less of showing the feature and more of showing the complexity. We are not trying to train them on the use of the product, just showing the value!

Ex: *Click* Look at that, the pen nib is out! *Click* Now it's gone again and ready for pocket storage, no protector needed!

Tell #2 - Bring home the Value

The main difference between Tell #1 and #2 is talking about the value that this feature brings to the user. Reiterate what you just did and then hammer in what value that functionality brings. Having prepped them with 'Tell #1,' they understand what the need is and now they can internalize the values that it brings.

Ex: "I just walked you through the click functionality. With that patented 'Click-n-Hide' technology you are able to spend far less time removing pen caps and get right to taking notes. When you are done just click and go without the need to find the missing cap and without the potential cost of nasty ink stains."

Boom. Value.

There you go, 'Tell-Show-Tell' becomes 'Need-Show-Value'. Explain the need, show the feature, describe the value. Ideally, at the end of your demo, you go over the X number of these TST type modules you covered and hit on their values one more time. Meta 'Tell-Show-Tell'. Cap off the demo with any questions and you are ready to go.

By performing your demos in this way you gain several significant benefits. Tell #2 automatically forces you to pause after a logical section in your demo. That pause gives the prospect time to absorb what you just said, think of any questions, and lets you mentally prep for the next module. It also stops their mental stopwatch. You know that part of your brain that runs when someone is talking at you where the longer it runs, the less you care. They didn't see 45 minutes of features, they saw several 3-5 minute value propositions.

That is really the crux of it. Give your prospect one value to take away per module. The end of the demo comes and they take away several values your software provides. We Sales Engineers too often get caught up in trying to train people during the demo. Don't do that. They should leave with the knowledge of those values to support their decision, not attempting to remember nearly an hour of 'How-Tos'.

HOW YOU SAY IT MATTERS

When presenting a software demo via the web, you lose out on a lot of good information in the room. Who is sitting there, what their non-verbal reactions are, the level of interest, etc. What we tend to forget is that the people on the other end of the phone have lost that too! They can't see how animated you are when you talk about an individual value of your software, they can only hear what you say and how you say it.

What you say is a small portion of communication. I don't believe that it is only 7% as some studies suggest, but it isn't everything by far. How you say those words is crucial. Delivery is a huge factor when doing a web presentation because the only tools you have to hold an audience's attention are what you say, how you say it, and what is on your screen. The 'How' is where great presentations go to die.

Regardless if your product is the most amazing thing since sliced bread, how you deliver that content will make or break the presentation. You need to be able to speak in such a way that the recipients actually hear what you are saying not how you say it.

Wait, didn't I just say that 'How' is the most important part? I'm flip flopping more than [insert today's top political candidate]! What you want to say is dependant on how you say it. If your 'How' is horrible can you really expect people to pay attention to the 'What'?

So how can you get out of the way of what you are trying to say? There are a couple of areas that I like to keep an ear on when doing a presentation.

1) Verbal Graffiti - Vocalized Silences and Crutch Phrases

I talked briefly about this in the previous chapters. This is the easiest area of improvement to notice and one of the most difficult to replace. If you have 'ums' and 'uhhs' peppered through your demo they break the flow of your story. People will have a hard time hearing a value if every third word is 'um'. Furthermore, if you have your favorite catchphrases everywhere, "and things of that nature", "moving on", "excellent", people will start noticing those words instead of the content.

The first way to fix this is to become aware. Record your next demo and then immediately afterward, listen to it. Yes, it will be hard, just do it. Take note every time you say 'um', look for the same phrases that repeat. Note all of them and you will be surprised how many are there. Just for fun divide the time of your presentation by the 'ums' and find out how often it happens. One every couple of seconds is very common and very distracting.

Once you are aware, the simple fix is to just breathe. Before you start your sentence take a deep breath. Formulate your thoughts and go. Whenever you feel an 'um' coming on, pause briefly, breathe, and continue. You will never, nor should you, get rid of all graffiti. Demos should not fall prey to the Newscaster Accent. In conversations and life 'uh' happens, just not too often to become distracting.

2) Tortoise and the Hare - Delivery Speed

Most people have one of two speed settings when doing a demo, Ludicrous Speed or Sloth Mode. You get started, get to your speed, and that is where you stay the entire time. Perfect for the highway but bad for a dcmo.

We are trying to get our message across to the audience. If you stay at the same speed, you give everyone watching the opportunity to check out. Think of listening to your history teacher drone on in a death march. By varying your cadence, the demo starts to feel more natural, more like a conversation. It also holds people's attention. Every change in speed naturally drags people back into what you are saying.

Even further than just modifying your speed, you need to be conscious of how quickly you are speaking. Even slow-talkers will frequently present at a brisk clip. The upside is you get more words per minute; the downside is your audience doesn't get a chance to digest what you are telling them. Presentations should always be around 80% of normal speaking cadence. Take a deep, measured breath, and then start talking. It may feel uncomfortable to you but the person listening will have a much easier time following along.

More straightforward to follow means more likely to listen. Capiche?

3) Pitch Perfect - Monitor your tone

The above also goes for pitch. Think about that history teacher again. One constant speed of delivery and the same monotone voice for a whole hour. It is enough to bore anyone to tears. People buy on emotion, just not that emotion.

When you start talking more quickly, you will naturally begin to speak at a higher pitch. Give it a try, force yourself to speed up and feel your voice lift. Slow down and hear how your tone gets deeper. Listen to your recording from the previous steps and, this time, pay attention to the delivery speed and pitch. These exercises will give you the ability to modulate at will and start working it into your demo.

To experiment with working on these skills, you can start small. Pick one area of your demo, one feature, one value, and put a sticky note on your monitor labeled with that one topic. When you get to that portion put excitement into your voice, talk faster, raise your voice! Those emotions will bleed through and infect your audience, pulling them back into your demo. Variation is key!

4) Break it down

Finally, stop talking. Just do it. People have an internal stopwatch that starts ticking when you start yakking. That timer doesn't stop until you do. We don't control it, it is just there. Unfortunately, that means it controls us.

When you talk for 30 minutes straight then stop and ask for questions, their stopwatch finally stops. Their brain isn't separating what you said into the six logical chunks that you went through, it is one big memory that they are trying to process. Like force feeding your toddler an entire Weetabix biscuit. I've tried it, doesn't work.

A human brain is an amazing organ capable of feats we can barely comprehend. It is also fairly simple to work with. Break your demo down into smaller sections, no more than 5-7 minutes each. Pause at the end of each section. Not just 'stop and ask for questions', actually take a beak for a good several seconds. Give their stopwatch a chance to reset and their brain time to process everything you just said. Now ask for questions, one more pause, move on. The 'Tell-Show-Tell' method really helps here.

CHEAT CODES FOR WEB DEMOS

Before we move onto some more of the management focused topics, I would like to share with you a few ways that you can cheat in your demos. These are all useful in general demos, but much more impactful on web based demos.

As mentioned in previous chapters a majority of communication is lost by doing remote presentations. Unfortunately, we live in a world where doing a face-to-face demo for all prospects is impossible. Would I love to travel the world on the company dime? Absolutely! Is it the smartest way to be a good steward of budget? Probably not.

With that we are stuck doing web demonstrations which strips our communication down to two things. What is one your screen and what you are saying, at the single point in time. We only have those two tools at our side to get our story across. So we need to take every shortcut available to get an advantage. Here are some of my tried and true cheats that I've used to great success.

Mouse Size Matters

First we deal with what is on your screen. Assuming your app doesn't have a ton of whirlygigs and dancing bananas, there won't be much motion. Motion naturally attracts the eye, allowing you to draw attention to certain areas. The bold section above gives away what I'm about to say but your mouse cursor is your greatest ally (or biggest nemesis).

First, regardless of what magics you cast on your cursor, moving too quickly will destroy every good effect you are trying for. We know where we are about to move the mouse so we know where to look. When your cursor disappears from where the prospect is looking, they start wandering around your screen without seeing what you are pointing at. So move slowly!

Now that you have slowed down you can further these efforts by changing your cursor icons. A small white pointer isn't the best, so go for the opposite! Personally I use an extra-large, black pointer. You can change your entire pointer style set on the OS level. Larger and darker cursors are going to allow for much easier viewing.

Artistic Freedom

Adding to your mouse cursor you can draw on your screen. Not with sharpies but with other tools. Most web meeting software has some type of screen drawing capability. I use a Windows tool called ZoomIt.

Drawing on your screen gives you more ability to focus attention. That is what we are fighting against, people's natural tendency to not pay attention. I have three kids, I have a lot of experience in these matters.

When you have one specific area of your app that you are talking about, zoom in on it or draw a box around it. Again we are dealing with psychology here. Putting a box around something focuses attention on that one spot. Prospects are less likely to start looking at other portions of your app if you have literally framed the discussion. Attention to you means retention of what you are saying!

Cleanliness is next to Godliness

No, you don't need to shower before each demo. I'm talking about cleaning up your demo environment. Nothing is more interesting to a demo watcher than everything on your screen other than your solution. My favorite is reading peoples email and chat notifications.

Give your demo every chance at success. Remove these unneeded (at the time) distractions. The easiest way to figure this out is to watch a recording of your demos. Pause the video every few minutes and highlight everything on screen that is not:

A) **Your app**
B) **Used in your demo at that moment**

Those are the only two things that you should be looking at. Anything else is a distraction to your prospect. Think about:

- Icons on your desktop other than your app
- Background – Simple plain color or your company logo
- System tray utilities – hide them all
- Tabs, tools, or bookmarks in your browser
  - Easy way to handle this, have one browser specific for presentations
- Chat programs, Email, etc.
  - Anything that causes popup notifications

Again, look at everything. Close down any unneeded apps to clear your taskbar. If you are using other tools as part of your presentation, drag them to a secondary monitor. Use programs like UltraMon to actually move them to a separate toolbar, or Fences to auto-hide your desktop icons. Keep it clean folks.

A LITTLE SMALL BUT VERY CLEAN

See how clean and simple that looks? No distractions other than what you introduce during your demo. Now compare that image to your desktop right now. See any differences?

Roadmaps, because I don't ask for directions

This is a simple one. At the very beginning of your demo let everyone know what you will cover. That's it.

Start your demo with a slide presentation. Not the standard 50 slide corporate deck, put that one back in the archives. I opt for a two slide show. First slide has your company name, product logo, your name, title, and picture. Get a nice quality photo too, not one from a night on the town. A simple picture immediately turns you from a voice in the ether to a real human.

Second slide, what you will be going over in the demo. Just a simple bullet list with one line per bullet. Big text as well! No paragraphs here. Allow your prospects to know what you will be showing them and how long it will take. You get a double impact by doing this. You put them in a frame of reference for where they are during your demo, and you also get a chance to clarify that what you are covering is actually what they are looking for!

You had me at Yes

Another simple one, gotta love those. This is more of a preventative measure when someone asks a question on if you have specific functionality. Assuming the answer is yes (please, please never lie), just respond appropriately with a resounding Yes!.

Now stop. Just do it. Restraint is key with this one. You are likely already jumping to the portion of the app to show this functionality and have derailed the next few minutes of your demo, if not a lot more.

Say yes and then pause. Then ask if that is sufficient or do they need to see the specific widget in action. Most of the time people will just say they are set and you can get back to business.

Free Parking

Now onto a follow-up from just saying yes but also including just about any other question. Instead of being ok with just a yes the prospect wants to see that feature. Time to make a snap judgement; will this detour upset your demo? If not just go for it. If it will, time to bring in free parking.

Let the prospect know that you are happy to answer their question but would like to park it until the end of the demo to make sure you can cover everything needed. At this point simply drag a notepad window onto your screen and type out the question.

Another two-fold benefit here folks. First, you are proving that you will actually follow up at the end of the demo. At worst you have the note so that you can do research after the call. Second, it gives the viewers a chance to see your interpretation of their question. This allows them to clarify if you don't have it just right.

There you have it everyone. Six really simple cheat codes that you can use during your presentations to give you every chance at success. Remove the chaff and enjoy the wheaty morsels of your value-based demo.

MEASURING PRESENTATION SKILL

"My Sales Engineer team is amazing. They always crush their demos, prospects love them, they know everything!!!"

Above is a quote that I have heard ad nauseum from the salespeople who have worked with me when I was slinging demos full time and one that I now hear about the SEs I have trained. It makes me feel good inside. This statement is not unique to my padawan learners either. Most sales people I talk to love their SE team.

Sweet. We Sales Engineers have cornered the market in being amazing. The problem is how do you quantify being 'a superhero'? How do I, objectively, present growth of an SE to my boss when I want to give them a raise? I'm not sure about you, but if I went to my VP and said "This person deserves a raise. They were amazing and now have progressed to awesome based solely on my opinion."…. it probably wouldn't go well.

Even trying to take opinion out of the equation, what do you measure on? Number of demos? Closed won deals touched? Number of drinks the sales team bought them? No! These are not accurate reflections of the growth of an SE. Sure if they did 2x the number of demos of last year they did more work. Did that work result in any sales? Did they get better at doing that work? What happened?

In my first SE management gig, I had inherited a team of stellar Sales Engineers and set out to begin training them to become better. Better how? Better at what? How would I know if they improved? There was no way to objectively quantify their skills. Since I couldn't measure them, I couldn't train them.

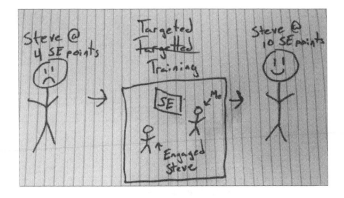

First, I had to look at the What. Using the famous Magic Quadrants of Sales Engineering, I tried to figure out what is the common theme among us. Regardless if you are heavy on the tech side, leaning more towards sales, or just churning out endless rote demos, we all do presentations. Presenting is the core of the Sales Engineer. However 'presentation skills' are not very easily measured. I'm pretty good at speechifying at people, but how can I take what I do naturally and train someone else on it?

Let's take a quick break here to clarify two words that I will overuse in this post:

Objective: Based on fact. Not influenced by personal opinion or feelings.
Quantify: To quantify something.

Ok, back to the story. If there was no way for me to measure one of my cherished staff, I had no way to lead them to be a greater Sales Engineer. My desire to train them and pass on my skills as an orator was squashed like so many villagers when the dragon is roused. Poor villagers.

My next task was to figure out how someone can be graded on presenting something. It wasn't fair to say that one person is a level 3 speaker and one is a level 4 if I myself did not know what would make me a 10. With that, I endeavored to break the act of 'presenting' down into smaller particles. The list I came up with is as follows (in no particular order):

Objection Handling - Can you deal with interruptions?

Tell-Show-Tell Mastery - Details in the previous section.

Cadence - How well you manage the speed and pitch of delivery.

Vocalized Silences - Umms, uhhs, 'you know', 'things of that nature'.

Unscripted Style - Here is a topic, speak for 5 minutes.

Time Management - Managing a call to the time allotted.

Value Props - Ability to respond with values instead of features.

Each of these skill levels was then broken down into four levels. I used 0-3 because I got a comp sci degree and zero based counting is forever ingrained in my mind. You could use 1-4. Don't get crazy and do 1-5 though that would destroy the whole system. The reason it would? It is based on the four stages of competency. Unconsciously incompetent, Consciously incompetent, Consciously competent, Unconsciously competent.

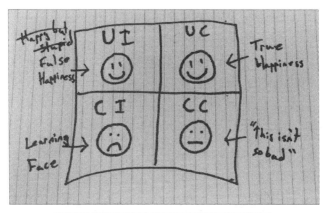

HIS HAPPINESS IS BORN OF IGNORANCE

Basically, you don't know what you don't know, you are aware of what you don't know, you consciously know it, then you know it so well it happens, wait for it, unconsciously. If you aren't familiar with the four stages, I highly recommend hopping on the interwebs and giving it a gander.

With that basic outline, I was able to take my rubric on grading presentation skills from opinion to a quantifiable and objective measurement. I interviewed each of my staff and watched their presentations. Then, using my rubric, I graded them in their mastery of the seven components of presenting. All of a sudden I had a baseline for which to measure their growth!

The second part, which is most important to my style of management, was to have the SE watch their own demo and then grade themselves. They were provided with my rubric, each of the seven areas with four levels of skill that were highly detailed. This was done prior to me sharing how I graded them. It is a lot easier for someone to accept an area of growth if they come to that conclusion themselves. We would then be able to have a good conversation about any grades that were drastically different. The measure of success I had setup for my rubric though was that when followed, there shouldn't be any difference. Luckily I did my job well and the rubric worked. Everyone graded themselves the same way I did. Management points!

From there it is very easy to pinpoint what skills your team needs to work on collectively and individually. Use the common themes to do team based training. Have them play some presentation games, impromptu speeches, communication exercises, etc. Afterward, break them into individual training. Focus on one skill each month to work on. The easiest way to do this is to record demos and have both the manager and SE watch and grade their level of that one skill.

At the end of the year, you will be able to look objectively at your team and show actual growth in the different skill levels. That is the type of information you can use to show improvements! Below is the rubric, feel free to customize it to suit your team's needs.

Presentation Skill Level	Objection Handling	Tell-Show-Tell	Cadence	Vocalized Silence	Value Props	Unscripted Style	Time Management
0	Questions and interruptions derail demo.	Does not use this method.	Presentations are consistently faster than normal speaking cadence.	Every sentence has VSes or CPs. Does not realize when it is happening.	Does not know value props.	Not able to speak without preparation.	Unable to perform a scripted demo within 30 minutes. Either drastically long or short.
1	Able to park questions to follow up after a call but not answer during the demo.	Able to perform basic tell-show-tell with a scripted demonstration on some sections.	Presentations are faster than normal speaking cadence but can be slowed down. After slowing down speeds back up.	Most sentences have VSes or CPs. Aware of which CPs are used and can note VS usage.	Understands and can communicate the functionality of the app.	Able to perform a level 1-2 presentation on a random topic with no preparation. Able to point out flaws in presentation after.	Able to cover most material of a scripted demo but has to cut or shorten sections to finish on time, or draw out remaining sections to fill it.
2	Able to answer feature based questions during a demo.	Able to perform tell-show-tell on standard presentations for most sections.	Demonstrations are done at normal speaking cadence. When cadence begins to speed up it is noted and slowed down.	Able to perform a demo with few VSes/CPs. Able to pick up on new CPs as they begin to form.	Able to talk about the benefits that the features bring.	Able to perform a level 2-3 presentation on a random topic with no preparation.	Manages demo to cover all scripted material within 45 minutes while handling QA.
3	Able to seamlessly handle all objections and continue demo without issue.	Natively uses the tell-show-tell method when presenting/answering QA/troubleshooting.	Presentations are performed slightly slower than a normal speaking cadence and is naturally regulated.	VSes nearly eliminated from normal presentations. CPs are not repeated more than twice in a presentation.	Audible ready to present relevant values to a customer based on their before scenarios.	Able to perform a 5 minute level 4 presentation with no preparation.	Able to perform a successful demo of a tool regardless of time allotted. Handles expectations and keeps demo on time.

METRICS THAT MATTER

The previous section covers how to measure the growth of your SE team's presentation skills. Now it is time to start measuring their output. Typically people will turn to widgets produced and put a metric around that, but # of SE work units is not always the best metric to roll up to the top because it doesn't mean anything useful. An SE typically does 100% of the demos requested. If that total number is lower, are they not meeting expectations? What metrics are actually useful?

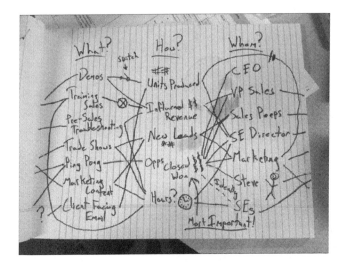

Unfortunately, that depends on to whom you roll up those numbers. Clearly we are doing our work and crushing it. To people who are reading the metrics however, they may only be seeing numbers. The problem isn't what to record but what do you want to portray to people not monitoring your day to day? Here you are making a sale to your boss instead of a prospect, meaning you want a great story. We need to take what we do and correlate it to success criteria pertinent to our line of business. Once we have done that it provides a two-fold benefit: keeping the higher ups informed about our value AND backs us up when we ask for another hire.

Alright, let's break this out into our most important tasks and how best to track it. Note: This is based on what I do with my team, your mileage may vary. These are fairly standard SE metrics but modify them to what is pertinent to your business model.

Product Demonstrations and Troubleshooting for Prospects

The core of what we do as Sales Engineers are presentations. We need to track how many but can't stop there. Number of demos per week brings us the ability to hire more people as we reach peak SE usage assuming we are effectively leveraging those people. I could just tell the sales people to jam every lead into a demo and max out my staff. Does that mean I need to hire more people? No, it means I'll have a lot of full schedules, no-shows, low percentage of demo-to-close, and unhappy staff. Do that long enough and I definitely will need to hire, hire replacements for my burnt out staff.

How many demos a week can an SE do? In my experience if a Sales Engineer is doing 15-20 qualified demos a week they are at capacity. After 20, you are spending less time preparing and you begin down the path of the Demo Jockey. If that is the model of your team, then numbers of demos is the only metric you need. To branch into other styles of SEs you should start looking at the following ideas. Baseline: get the number of demos tagged to opportunities. Next step: extrapolate info from that data.

Number of demos is the basis of what you record. Where you record those is the key though. These demos should be tracked against opportunities! My team usually does not do a demo for a prospect unless the salesperson thinks there is an opportunity there. Why waste precious resources if the sales perp doesn't think there are dollars to hunt? With opp data, we can say 'Steve did 15 demos last week. Those demos touched $352k in pipeline.' Sweet!

Do this for a quarter and you can go to your boss and say 'Steve did 114 demos this quarter, influencing $863k in new closed won business.'! You can't tell me that the CEO is going to doubt your team's value when you start rolling up those kinds of numbers. Mostly because you can correlate that info even further.

- X amount of revenue was influenced by each SE
- Which salespeople are being most efficient with their application of SEs
- Close rate for any SE touched deal broken down by individual SE
- How many SE engagements are needed per opp
- How much revenue is impacted per SE engagement

All of this is great info for the SE, SE Director, and VP of Sales; allowing you to make decisions objectively about how to allocate the SE resources. You can also isolate people that may need more training, both Sales and SEs.

Trade Shows/On-site Visits

Marketing leans on their SE team. We provide that duality of technical cognition and sales acumen that they want at trade shows. Same goes for on-site visits to customers/prospects. You don't want to bring a developer to walk through the functionality, you need someone to help work the room and bring the technical and business values. However, these are costly propositions. An on-site visit takes 1-3 days of an SEs time (including travel) for one customer, where a trade show allows a few days of many quick conversations for leads at the very top of the funnel. One impacts only a single deal and the other impacts only potential opportunities.

These are costly and that means they need tracking. The way I handle this is by 'day'. Each day of travel is logged as one unit of travel. I leave on a Monday for CA, have a meeting on Tuesday, then head home Wednesday. Three travel units. Of course, these are all logged on the opportunity for financial tracking, but also useful for weighting against their other activities. An SE travels three days in one week, their demo numbers will be 2/5 what they normally are. The travel units allow us to build in expectations of dips in demo numbers which allow you to regulate actual per week averages of calls. Plus, at the end of the year, you can gauge how much time you spent on the road and plan for the coming years staffing needs.

Even further are the trade shows. If you have an incredible marketing team, they should be able to track the leads, opp value, and close rate from the convention conversations. The SE travel units can be aligned with these numbers to show "for each day an SE is at a conference, we generate XYZ amount of new pipeline which converts at #%.". I'm sure the marketing manager is going to care when they can pay an extra 15k to have an SE go to a trade show that generates 100k in new opps per day. Alternately if we prove that an SE provides no value at certain shows, we can save money and time by just sending a slide show. This keeps Sales people on the floor closing while SEs leverage the first half of their title to help generate some leads.

Other

The above are the main tasks that my SE teams have historically covered. We do a variety of other tasks that I measure like generating marketing content, customer facing emails, client relationship calls, services (if we get roped into it), etc. All of those things are tracked in terms of numbers, tagged to revenue if at all possible, and then weighted for time appropriately. All of these measurements are included in the numbers that I roll up to the top. Those metrics are all basic and easily understood which allows anyone to view them and have great insight into what we do, why it is valuable, and what trajectory is the department on.

In my opinion, any repeated task over an hour should be dutifully metric'd. It is the worst five minutes of your week spent tagging all your activity but boy, does it work wonders. You get to know exactly what you accomplished every week/month/year as an SE and exactly how much impact you had on the business. You may be surprised at how much value you or your team provides. Personally, I like being able to rattle off the number of demos I have done in my career and the total revenue I have influenced. Come on, I play video games. This is how I generate a high score for my career.

GENERIC SE PROFILE

The following is a set of profiles for Sales Engineers used during hiring. People who match this profile are great candidates for your first, or their first, SE position. I have them broken into an entry and high-level position, depending on what exactly you need. You will have great success using the entry-level profile for Demo Jockeys and new Sales Engineers. The high-level profile is ideal for a first Sales Engineer as well. Due to the technical nature of the Solution Architect, you should lean closer to the high-level profile strictly. Regardless, hand this profile to the person recruiting and tell them to look for these types of folks.

Entry Level SE Profile

- Previous Positions Held
  - Technical Support
  - Software Trainer
  - Professional Services
  - Technical Sales
  - Sales Support
  - Technical Marketing
  - QA Engineer
- Tasks they may have performed
  - Worked directly with customers or prospects
  - Learned software independently of job
  - Dealt with a high number of tasks on a daily basis
  - Represented their company at trade shows
  - Worked directly with Sales teams
  - Managed projects independently
  - Taught technical topics either in person or via the web
  - Done a webinar or some other web-based presentation

- Soft Skills they need to have
  - Learn new technology quickly
  - Work with people over the phone
  - Work autonomously as well as on a team
  - Proper written and verbal communication, both technical and non
  - Explain technical topics to non-technical audience
  - Deductive reasoning
  - Time management
  - Sales acumen
- Technologies they may have worked with
  - APIs
  - Current web technology
  - Software development tools
  - Backend server monitoring
  - Scripting in popular languages, Python, Ruby, etc
  - Any type of coding experience
  - Extensive Microsoft Office use, actual use not typing papers and pasting into Excel
  - Any product that your company sells

High-Level Sales Engineer Profile

- Previous Positions Held:
  - Software Trainer
  - Technical Sales
  - Professional Services
  - Internal Tech Support
  - Software Consultant
  - Support Services
  - Solutions Architect/Engineer
  - Sales Support/Consultant
  - Sales Trainer
  - Software Sales
- Skills and abilities they should have:
  - Ability to troubleshoot issues
  - Work with customers over the phone
  - Deductive reasoning and logic
  - Active listening
  - Ability to work cross-department
  - Accurately explain technical topics to both technical and non-tech people
  - Ability to speak in public
  - Creative content or technical writing
  - Work autonomously
  - Time management
  - Technical writing skills

- o Broad exposure to technology
- o Ability to prioritize tasks effectively
- o Willingness to help out
- o Sales acumen
- o Honesty
- o Great personality
- Things they may have done:
  - o Provided technical support
  - o Worked directly with clients on software implementation
  - o Managed workload of a small team of technical staff
  - o Worked in a high-velocity environment, higher amount of tasks over shorter bursts of time
  - o Worked in an environment that responds to urgent requests
  - o Deployed a process or program to customers or internally
  - o Worked as part of a team to increase efficiency of something
  - o Be solely responsible for high-level projects
  - o Public speaking experience
  - o Worked directly with a sales organization
  - o Trained people on software

o   Represented technical products at an industry
    event
o   Designed client facing documentation
o   Pre and Post-sales customer management

How Do You Compensate Them

Compensation is always a difficult topic to broach, especially for new positions. How do you best motivate your Sales Engineer to help sales hit their number while still providing enough incentive for highly competent technical staff? I have come across a variety of ways, some great and some pretty terrible for everyone involved. Comp plans really depend on the structure of your sales department already.

The first thing to note is that regardless of your comp plan, a Sales Engineers plan should be majority base pay. The best splits are in the 70/30 to 80/20 range of base to variable. With these kinds of splits you are able to accurately compensate a technical asset for their skills in helping with the sale while removing the risk of too much variable component, which can cause SEs to drop the 'trusted advisor' role and do whatever it takes to close a deal.

The variable component needs to be timely as well. Your Sales Engineers should be getting their bonus paid out, at least, every quarter, if not every time you run commissions. Waiting for a mid-year or end-of-year bonus removes the high that comes after a successful quarter. It also removes the severity of a bad quarter. SEs should share in both the highs and the lows.

Comp plans don't just reward activity on sales either. When your SE is tightly aligned with the number, they will start going above and beyond to get more deals closed. For Sales reps, they will make more calls, gin up more business from their territory, etc. Sales Engineers will be working with marketing to generate more traffic and trials, participating in the industry to get more brand awareness, find any possible means to get more leads in the hands of the reps and increase the size of the opps that arise.

Finally, don't put a cap on the total commissions. Sure, cap individual deals if you do commission sharing, but not the total amount an SE can earn. Nothing is more of a disincentive than getting to September and realizing that you aren't getting anything more for the rest of the year. Time to phone it in for a few months or take a long holiday... Below are two of the best ways to get your SEs in line with the goal.

Commission Sharing

One of the easiest ways to get an SE on board with hitting the number, give them a portion of all sales they work on. Find some percentage of the deals that will equitably reward your SE and go for it. If this is your first SE, you may not know how many deals they will touch, estimate that 80-90% of the deals will require assistance. At this point, the SE is incentivized to assist on every deal possible and ensure they close. Without any cap on this, your SE will spend their free time figuring out how to get more deals into the pipeline. This is as direct a tie as you can get and is the ideal way to incentivize them.

Why isn't this the only way I recommend then? This is **only** possible if you have one SE per team. More than one SE supporting a sales team and now you have people fighting for demos, multiple SEs being tagged in an opportunity, and difficulty distinguishing what level of involvement deserves a reward. The last thing you want is to pit SEs against each other or against the sales team.

This type of comp plan lends itself nicely to being paid out on the same schedule as your sales commissions. A deal closes and the next commission both the rep and the SE are able to celebrate. A deal falls through and the team is incentivized to dig in harder for the next pay period.

Ex: $50,000 deal closes – Rep gets 5% ($2500) - SE gets 0.5% ($250)

Bonus based on team goals

This is my second favorite way of setting up a comp plan. It allows multiple SEs to support a single sales team and still be actively tied to the goal. The premise is that your SE has their variable pay component tied directly to the sales teams number for the quarter. At that point, each of your SEs is incentivized to do everything possible for their entire team, reps and other SEs included.

By basing everything on the team number, you remove the issue of SEs fighting over accounts. Each SE will be more likely to hop on any call to help it close. It also creates a great sense of comradery for your group as they will constantly be working to improve the whole team, not just themselves. Warning, numbers incoming.

Many people argue for a straight payout. 80% of the number garners 80% of the bonus, 120% equals 120% bonus, etc. The main issue with this is that it divorces the SE from caring too greatly about the number depending on the bonus potential. For example: on a $20k yearly bonus breaking out to $5k quarterly you pay out $4k for 80% of the number, $5k at 100%, $6k at 120%. A $2000 swing for 20% above or below goal isn't that bad, but isn't that good either, especially considering that 20% above or below is a significant range that is either getting salespeople promoted or fired respectively.

Now look at the close numbers. 96% of your goal nets you $4800 and 100% gets you to $5000. As an SE I don't really care if we get to 96% because I got the majority of my bonus. More would be nice of course, but I'm not going to work 12 hour days at the end of the quarter to get an extra hundred bucks.

To alleviate this issue, I like to use positive and negative accelerators. Warning, even more, numbers incoming:

- 0 - 75% = No bonus payout
- 75% - 85% = - 25% of bonus potential
- 85% - 90% = -10% of bonus potential
- 90% - 100% = Full bonus potential
- 100% - 110% = Full bonus potential plus 2x bonus percentage per point
- 110%+ = Full bonus potential plus 3x bonus percentage per point
  - o Max accelerator would be capped at 150%

- **Examples – Based on quarterly bonus of 10k**
  - Number hit
    - **0-74%**
      - No bonus payout - ☹
    - **75%**
      - Bonus potential = 75% of 10k with a 25% negative accelerator
      - $7500 – 25% = **$5625 total bonus after $1875 penalty**
    - **85%**
      - Bonus potential = 85% of 10k with a 10% negative accelerator
      - $8500 – 10% = **$7650 total bonus after $850 penalty**
    - **90%**
      - Bonus = 90% of 10k with no penalty
      - **$9000 total bonus**
    - **105%**
      - Bonus = 105% of 10k + additional 10% (2x overage percentage of 5%)
      - $10,500 + 10% = **$11,550 total bonus after $1050 bonus bonus**
    - **115%**

- Bonus = 115% of 10k + additional 45% (3x overage percentage)
- $11,500 + 45% = **$16,675 total bonus after $5175 bonus bonus**
  - **200% (High company overachievement)**
    - Bonus = 200% of 10k + additional 150% (3x overage percentage at cap)
      - o Cap locks accelerator at 150% instead of 3x100% or 300%
    - $20,000 + %150 = **$50,000 total bonus after $30k bonus bonus**
      - o **Would be 80k without cap**

Now you really have incentivized your team to get into the next tier. Just like each rep is fighting to get into their personal accelerators, now your SEs and Sales Managers are working to push the whole department number into the stratosphere. I doubt your CEO will mind paying a massive bonus to your stellar SEs when they get to present 200% of plan to the board.

CONCLUSION

Assuming you didn't 'choose-your-own-adventure'
yourself all the way to this page, thank you for reading
my book. This collection of stories and tips has come
from many years of Sales Engineering, both on the
ground and building teams. It is my hope that
everyone who reads this book is able to learn a bit
more about this, the best career in the world. Whether
you are in your first SE role, hiring your first SE, or
just realizing that what you have been doing is
engineering sales all along, you are part of a growing
industry of like-minded individuals. Welcome to the
club.

\- Gregg -

Roll Credits

| • |

Made in the USA
San Bernardino, CA
03 August 2017